Seasonal Activities for Classroom Creativity

Content-Based No Fail Exercises

by Kitty Y. Hazler

Incentive Publications, Inc.
Nashville, Tennessee

ACKNOWLEDGMENT

To Richard, who always believed.

Illustrated by Gayle S. Harvey
Cover by Becky Rüegger
Edited by Jennifer E. Janke

ISBN 0-86530-431-9

Table of Contents

To The Teacher

This collection of activities for fourth through sixth graders is designed to provide practice in creative behaviors. Activities include creative behaviors from the cognitive domain (fluency, flexibility, originality, and elaboration) and from the affective domain (risk taking, complexity, curiosity, and imagination).

Materials are designed with your busy classroom in mind—a minimum of author text and a maximum of things for you to use. Each *Suggestions for Use* page provides ways to introduce, supplement, and conclude activities. These activities need not be graded and can be used by the whole class, small groups, or individual students to provide thinking practice and to help students develop new skills.

There is a seasonal nature to the activities, but many may be adapted to use at any time of year. Use them when you need them and in whatever order you need them.

Each of us has the potential to be a creative individual. Sometimes we need a jump-start to get us thinking and behaving creatively. These activities provide your students with added practice that encourages creativity—both theirs and yours.

Enjoy!

January—Start The Year Off Right...

This activity asks students to be **flexible** as they think about different events in each month of the year. **Originality** in thinking is important.

Ask your students if they made any New Year's resolutions. The start of a new year makes people think about what they can do to make their lives better. Your students may have big hopes for the year, and now is a good time for them to think about what they can do to fulfill their hopes for January and beyond. Ask your students to write their hopes for each month.

Do one month with the students. December might be easier for them, because they automatically think of holidays. Brainstorm ideas about what makes December "fine," and write them on the board. Be sure to join in the conversation yourself. The students will be interested in what you have to share.

Remind the class not to focus only on holidays, even though that is sometimes easier. What else happens throughout the year? Think about vacations, competitions, sports, family traditions, school, and maybe even something they've never tried before.

Share ideas when the assignment is finished. Each student could share one idea they wrote that they thought was original.

January–Start The Year Off Right

It's always good to begin a new year on a positive note, and it would be nice to be able to manipulate events to make sure that each month is great.

On the calendar below, show what you could do each month to make that month great for yourself.

January	**July**
February	**August**
March	**September**
April	**October**
May	**November**
June	**December**

Name _____ Date _____

Seasonal Activities for Classroom Creativity

January Is...

This activity asks students to be **original** and **imaginative**. They also use **elaboration** when they add details.

Begin the activity by asking students what they think poetry is. It's great if they come up with some actual poetry forms like couplets or Haiku. If they don't, keep things simple with rhymed poetry and unrhymed poetry.

Ask students for examples of poems they know. They can name some of their favorite poems.

This would be an appropriate time to explain what free verse is. Try some free verse together as a group. Animals are a good topic for practice with the group.

Try: **An elephant is . . .** (a big wrinkled gray blanket)
   Ants are . . .
   A leopard is . . .
   A puppy is . . .

Work as a group, and remind students to try to create a very vivid word picture.

Sharing free verse when the assignment is completed gives everyone a sense of closure, and it's fun to listen to the variety of responses.

The students can copy their favorite *January Free Verse* on plain white paper, which can then be mounted on blue construction paper. Add a few snowflakes, and you have a January bulletin board.

January Is...

Free verse is a type of unrhymed poetry. One kind of free verse is written in a definition format with original and creative ideas for the definition.

Example:

January is . . . shivers and goosebumps in the morning.

Complete the following *January Free Verse.*

Icicles are . . .

Snowstorms are . . .

Hot cocoa is . . .

Frost is . . .

Fireplaces are . . .

Snow shoveling is . . .

Mittens are . . .

Sledding is . . .

Cold is . . .

January is . . .

Name _____ Date _____

Seasonal Activities for Classroom Creativity

Chilly Problems

This activity asks students to be **flexible** by looking at math word problems in a new way. Normally a word problem provides all the information a student will need to solve it. This activity provides students with data, and students must come up with the mechanics and format themselves. The challenge to take alternative actions means students are also working with **complexity**.

This activity also provides a way to introduce creative writing into the math curriculum.

If this is the first time the students have approached this type of activity, give them a practice run with other facts. Try the sample below together, and point out the wide range of possibilities for problems that you can make with one set of facts.

Sample facts:

15 boys	32 desks
12 girls	30 chairs
1 teacher	35 math books

Sample problem:

Ms. Jones' class has 27 students in it. Draw a diagram showing how 27 desks could be arranged for small group work. All the groups should be equal.

Share some of the problems when the students have completed the assignment. See what variety you have by tallying the number of addition, subtraction, multiplication, and division problems. Use the data you have collected, and have the students graph the information (picture, bar, and line). This can be done individually or in groups.

Chilly Problems

Using the facts given below, construct two (2) different interesting math word problems. All the facts need not be used in each problem, and you may bring more facts into your problem if you choose.

8 snowmen	24 hats
6 children	3 sleds
5 pairs of mittens	10 days of vacation
3 unmatched mittens	4 pairs of ice skates

Name _____ Date _____

Seasonal Activities for Classroom Creativity

Mission Improbable

This assignment asks students to be **flexible** by looking at Groundhog Day and animals in different ways. They should be using **original** ideas and their **imaginations** too. **Risk taking** is also involved when students are asked to defend their choices.

Before handing out this assignment, find out what the students know about Groundhog Day.

Groundhog Day Facts:

- It is celebrated on February 2.
- If Punxsutawney Phil, a famous groundhog from Punxsutawney, PA, comes out of his hole (after hibernation) and sees his shadow, then we are supposed to have six more weeks of winter weather.
- If the groundhog doesn't see his shadow, then we should have an early spring.
- A prognosticator is someone who makes predictions.

Compare choices when the class finishes the assignment. Were there any duplications? Which animal does the class, as a whole, feel would be the most creative choice to replace Phil?

Mission Improbable

It's February 1st, the day before Groundhog Day, and Punxsutawney Phil, the Groundhog Prognosticator, has just issued a statement for the press. The statement is as follows:

"I'm a tired old groundhog and all this fuss every February has just worn me out. I think a nice warm climate will be good for these old creaky bones, so I'm retiring and moving to Florida. If you want to continue all this February Foolishness, you're going to have to find somebody to take my place."

Your mission is to find a replacement animal for Punxsutawney Phil *immediately*. Consider the entire animal kingdom, and decide upon the best replacement for Phil. Select an animal and defend your choice with four (4) reasons as to why your decision is best.

Choice: _____

Reasons your choice is best:

1. _____
   _____
   _____

2. _____
   _____
   _____

3. _____
   _____
   _____

4. _____
   _____
   _____

Name _____ Date _____

Seasonal Activities for Classroom Creativity

Wanted: Valentine Perfection

This activity asks students to be **original** and to use their **imaginations.**

The children might share how they feel when they get a card or gift and also how they feel when they are the gift giver. Which do they like better, being the giver or receiver?

You can supply some newspaper classified ads for the children to examine and share with each other, so that everyone will have a feeling for the elements of a classified ad.

When the assignment is completed, students can exchange ads with each other and check to see if the ads are in a reasonable ad format. Students can then type or print the ads as a part of a bulletin board display.

Wanted: Valentine Perfection

Valentine's Day comes each year on February 14, with Valentine cards, flowers, or candy. It would be wonderful if each of us could find the perfect Valentine—a pal, a pet, or a sweetheart.

This year we are taking no chances. **Write a newspaper want ad describing your perfect Valentine. You may want to check some newspaper ads for ideas before you begin.**

_____

_____

_____

_____

_____

_____

_____

_____

_____

_____

_____

_____

_____

_____

_____

_____

_____

_____

_____

Name _____ Date _____

Seasonal Activities for Classroom Creativity

Remembering Special Individuals

This task involves **complexity**, because students are asked to seek alternatives, and also some **risk taking**, because they must defend their choices.

It would be worthwhile to first find out what the students remember about George Washington and Abraham Lincoln. These findings could be summarized on a chalkboard. Then, ask the class why they think we happen to celebrate these two presidents' birthdays, when we don't celebrate other birthdays like Martin Van Buren's or Chester A. Arthur's.

Ask students to help you make a listing on the chalkboard of other holidays that honor an individual.

After completing the assignment, ask the students to pick their one favorite individual, and write the individual's name down on a piece of paper (this will help avoid mind-changing later). Let each student share the individual's name and the reason he or she chose that individual. Keep a tally on the board. It will be interesting to see how many duplicates there are.

A possible challenge to extend the assignment would to be to ask students to find out how one would go about creating a national holiday.

Remembering Special Individuals

In February we celebrate the birthdays of two presidents, Abraham Lincoln and George Washington, and in other months we remember many special people.

Choose five (5) other individuals whose lives you feel warrant a special day of remembrance. List the individuals below, and explain the reasoning behind your choices.

1. _____

_____

_____

2. _____

_____

_____

3. _____

_____

_____

4. _____

_____

_____

5. _____

_____

_____

Name _____ Date _____

Seasonal Activities for Classroom Creativity

Top O' The Morning To You

This activity encourages **flexibility**, because students are looking at St. Patrick's Day in a different way, and **fluency**, because students are asked to provide multiple responses.

Before beginning this activity, discuss the holiday of St. Patrick's Day.
- St. Patrick's Day is celebrated on March 17, the feast day of Saint Patrick, the patron saint of Ireland.
- Patrick was a fifth century missionary to Ireland, where he converted many of the Irish to Christianity.
- He used the shamrock to explain the idea of the Trinity.
- St. Patrick's Day is primarily a religious holiday in Ireland, while in the United States it is primarily a secular holiday.
- The first St. Patrick's Day celebration in the U.S. was in Boston in 1737.

How many of the students wear green on St. Patrick's Day? Why do they wear it?

When the assignment is finished, go over the responses together. Someone can list the responses on the board.

How fluent was the class? How difficult did they find this assignment? This might be the time to discuss the idea that it can be frustrating when we think we should have come up with more responses then we did. Remind students that just like we exercise our body, we can also exercise our mind, and that we will get better at these creative skills through practice.

Top O' The Morning To You

Each year St. Patrick's Day is celebrated on March 17th. It is time for "wearing o' the green," whether you are Irish or not.

Consider all the ways we celebrate St. Patrick's Day, and think about the myths that go along with the holiday. List below ways that St. Patrick's Day would be different if we celebrated the "wearing o' the blue" instead of "the green".

_____

_____

_____

_____

_____

_____

_____

_____

_____

_____

_____

_____

_____

_____

_____

_____

_____

_____

Name _____ Date _____

Seasonal Activities for Classroom Creativity

A Sense Of Spring

This activity involves **elaboration**, because students must expand on their basic concepts of the senses. The activity also involves **curiosity**, because students must do some reflective thinking about their perceptions.

Before handing out this assignment, ask the class to name the five senses and list several examples of how we use each sense.

Sharing some of the responses after the assignment gives students the opportunity to see the variety of answers possible.

To extend the assignment further, students can each choose one of their responses and imagine that they are describing this response to someone who cannot utilize that sense. Ask students to create detailed word pictures for their imagined person (elaboration). Tell them to be as specific as possible. After completing this additional task, ask them to describe any difficulties they had completing the task and how they might do it differently next time.

A Sense Of Spring

Spring is here, and our senses are alert to the changes taking place around us. Below is a list of our five senses. **Under each sense, list three ways in which that particular sense allows us to recognize spring.**

Taste

    1.   the taste of fresh strawberries _____

    2.   _____

    3.   _____

Sight

    1.   _____

    2.   _____

    3.   _____

Smell

    1.   _____

    2.   _____

    3.   _____

Hearing

    1.   _____

    2.   _____

    3.   _____

Touch

    1.   _____

    2.   _____

    3.   _____

Name _____ Date _____

Seasonal Activities for Classroom Creativity

A Lesson Learned

This activity involves **curiosity**, because students must do some reflective thinking and explore their thoughts about their own past. They must also use **elaboration** when describing past events. There may also be some **risk taking** involved if they choose to share some unflattering occurrence that happened previously.

Help the students to decide upon an outcome that they would want for the assignment. A "for instance" from your own past will probably be the best example you can share. If you can't think of your own example, you're welcome to share mine: I learned this lesson one rainy spring day. My sisters and I dared a younger sister to run to the corner in the rain. It seemed pretty harmless at the time. In the process, she stepped on a rusty nail that resulted in a trip to the doctor for a tetanus shot. It was one of those times when I didn't think through the consequences of my actions.

Tying the lesson learned to spring limits the time frame from which the students must choose. If you feel this is too difficult, open the topic up to a lesson learned at any time of year.

Admitting our own errors is difficult for any of us. Students will get more from this assignment if they use a personal event from their own past, but they may substitute a family event.

Share some of the "stories" after the assignment with the whole class. Students will feel more comfortable discussing their foibles when all are involved.

A question that might be brought up after the sharing would be, "Do the lessons we learn under circumstances like these always stay learned?" We all need to be reassured, occasionally, that making mistakes is a part of being human. We hope not to repeat mistakes, but sometimes we do.

A Lesson Learned

Our past experiences help shape what we are today. We learn lessons in life each day. Some lessons are more obvious to us than others, and sometimes the lessons we learned the "hard way" are easier to remember than the lessons we learned more pleasantly.

No doubt some of the lessons you've learned have stemmed from an event that occurred in the spring of the year. **Look back on** *springs past* **in your life, and focus on one event that helped you learn about life in some way. Describe that event, and tell what you learned from it.**

_____

_____

_____

_____

_____

_____

_____

_____

_____

_____

_____

_____

_____

_____

_____

_____

_____

_____

_____

Name _____ Date _____

Seasonal Activities for Classroom Creativity

April Alliteration

This alliteration activity requires using **originality** to come up with clever and novel combinations of words. **Fluency** skills develop as students come up with several words beginning with the same letter.

Before beginning the activity, ask students to give examples of alliteration that they know. If they get stuck, remind them of the tongue twisters they've heard—Peter Piper, She sells seashells, etc.

Try some alliteration together. See how many alliterative phrases the class can develop using the word *tiger*.

Keep a dictionary or thesaurus handy if you get stuck for a word.

Share responses when the assignment is finished. Which one did they find most difficult? Why do they think that is? Are vowels harder to use than consonants?

Students could each copy a favorite alliterative response on an umbrella shape or a raindrop shape, which could then be put together for an April bulletin board.

April Alliteration

Alliteration is the practice of beginning two or more words in a passage with the same letter or sound. It can be an effective tool in writing, because it catches the eye or ear. Examples of alliteration are: Ban the Bomb, pecks of pickled peppers, Boston Bruins, and Sesame Street.

Form examples of alliteration with each of the words listed below.

1. raindrops — <u>rotten raindrops are ruining recess</u> _____

2. spring — _____

    _____

3. April — _____

    _____

4. bird(s)— _____

    _____

5. grass— _____

    _____

6. baseball— _____

    _____

7. Easter— _____

    _____

8. storm(s)— _____

    _____

9. mud— _____

    _____

10. playground— _____

    _____

Name _____ Date _____

Seasonal Activities for Classroom Creativity

And That's The True Story

This activity involves students using **originality** as they develop a novel approach to why the Easter Bunny hides eggs. Students put their **imaginations** to use as they create the story. **Flexibility** is also used, because they must write the story from an unusual approach; the writers know the ending of the story. It is their job to develop the beginning and middle.

Help students who need a jump-start by looking at another myth or holiday story, and brainstorm an original story behind it. You might collectively develop a story around why Santa's reindeer fly or one as to why the Tooth Fairy collects teeth.

Encourage students to illustrate their stories. If you want to try something different, have the children use torn construction paper to complete the illustrations. You will need background construction paper, scrap construction paper, and glue. The students illustrate the story by tearing out all the items they want in the illustrations. No drawing instruments or scissors are used.

Display completed illustrations along with the stories around the room or on a bulletin board.

And That's The True Story

Many of our holidays have myths or stories that add fun and excitement to the holiday celebration. One of these myths celebrates the Easter Bunny who hides eggs and brings baskets full of goodies during the springtime each year.

Expand your thinking beyond the ordinary, and develop an original story about the Easter Bunny. Your story can take any direction you choose, but it should end with the words *"and that's why the Easter Bunny hides eggs."*

Name _____ Date _____

Seasonal Activities for Classroom Creativity

April Showers

This activity is designed to focus on **fluency** as students are asked to come up with as many flower names as they can. The second part of the assignment works on **flexibility** and **research skills**. Children will increase flexibility when they think of different ways of discovering flower names. The directions to the assignment do not stipulate that the student must use books to learn other flower names. Encourage your students to investigate a variety of sources.

Make sure students understand that they will not be "scored or marked" on the number of flowers they list on the front page of the assignment. This should be independently done and is just a check to see how many names they can think of on their own.

After students have completed the assignment, discuss the front page of the assignment. Ask students to mark the flowers that other people in the class listed. How many original answers were there? Next, talk with your students about their lists on the back of the page. Find out what kind of references students used to discover the names of flowers. How much variety was there?

Fluency exercises can be done in many ways. Your class may enjoy playing "Categories" as a way to improve fluency.
In the game of "Categories" all players sit in a circle. The players develop a rhythm by clapping their hands twice on their own thighs, then clap their hands together twice and then finally snap the fingers on their right hand and then snap the fingers on their left hand. The first player names a category on the finger snaps (for example: girl's names, cars, dogs, etc.). The players go around the circle naming, on the finger snaps, an example of the category. If a player fails to name an example when it is their turn, they move out of the circle. The next player in the circle begins the clapping again and names a different category on the finger snaps. The game continues until only one person remains.

April Showers

"April showers bring May flowers" or so the old saying goes. Spring is wonderful with its abundance of fresh, new colors.

List as many flower names as you can on this side of the paper. This will show how fluent you can be. Use resource books, talk to a classmate, or use other resources to learn more flower names. List these new names on the back of this sheet.

Name _____ Date _____

Seasonal Activities for Classroom Creativity

A Mother's Day (Or Father's Day) Miracle

Suggestions for Use

The activity asks students to be **flexible**. They must look at their relationships with their parents in a different light. Students will also need to be original as they try to come up with unusual responses. As student writers generate multiple responses, they practice being **fluent**. There is the possibility of some **risk taking** in this assignment too if students share personal information about themselves with others.

Brainstorm ideas on how the "invisibility miracle" came about before the students begin writing. This could warm them up to the topic and open up ideas for them. This might be an appropriate time to teach about *piggybacking*, where new ideas are built on ideas already generated.

When students are finished writing, ask them to pick their favorite idea to share with the class. This sharing can be a lot of fun.

Ask students to think about the ramifications of other people being able to be invisible at will: a teacher, a policeman, their brother or sister—or even a pet.

A Mother's Day (Or Father's Day) Miracle

How could this have happened? Nobody can understand it or explain it. On Mother's (or Father's) Day, parents all over your city developed the ability to become invisible for short periods of time. We have no idea how long this phenomena will last, but it sure has made us rethink some of our actions.

List as many ways as you can in which this ability will change your life.

1. You will no longer be able to say you "washed" your hands before dinner when you just held them under the water for a second.

2. _____

_____

_____

_____

_____

_____

_____

_____

_____

_____

_____

_____

_____

_____

_____

_____

_____

_____

Name _____ Date _____

Seasonal Activities for Classroom Creativity

Spring Sends Its Greeting: ACHOO!

Suggestions for Use

Curiosity is used in this assignment as students do some reflective thinking about living with allergies. They will also use **elaboration** as they expand on their basic thoughts. **Imagination** will come into play as they envision themselves in the various situations.

Ask the class how many have allergies. Ask students to tell you what they think an allergy is and to what things people could be allergic.

After students have finished writing, share some of the individual responses, especially to the last part of the assignment. What does the class think might cause the kind of allergies that would necessitate living in a plastic bubble? How do they feel about the quality of life for someone under these circumstances?

Spring Sends Its Greeting: ACHOO!

The world awakens from its winter rest, and the earth becomes dotted with splashes of green. The green begins to grow and flowers emerge. Pollen fills the air and our noses. ALLERGY ALERT! Let the sneezing begin!

Write a paragraph about having pollen allergies. If you have them, describe what your life is like this time of year. If you don't have allergies, imagine what it's like.

_____

_____

_____

_____

_____

_____

_____

_____

_____

_____

_____

_____

_____

_____

_____

Pollen allergies are an annoyance and an inconvenience, but modern medicine allows us to function fairly normally in spite of these allergies. A very few people have such severe allergies that they cannot function in a normal environment and must live in specially sealed rooms that allow no contaminates to enter. **Imagine what life would be like in that kind of environment. Write your imaginings on the back of this paper.**

Name _____ Date _____

May Play

Flexibility is a big part of this activity. Students must use a variety of approaches to come up with the solutions. This assignment also involves **complexity**, since students must organize their thoughts and look for alternative answers.

Hink Pinks are fun to do. Students will need very little practice to understand how to do them. Try the following samples together before you assign this activity:

> **A phony boa . . .** (fake snake)
>
> **A swamp filled with pigs . . .** (hog bog)
>
> **A cap for a rodent . . .** (rat hat)
>
> **A boiling pan . . .** (hot pot)

Answers to MAY PLAY:

1.	bee tree	6.	loose spruce
2.	rose hose	7.	stern fern
3.	numb mum	8.	grass lass
4.	tame flame	9.	toss moss
5.	fine vine	10.	leaf thief

Once students feel comfortable with the idea, they'll be able to create their own hink pinks. Sharing their creations with the class gives everyone a chance to shine.

For more fun try hinky pinkys, two syllable rhyming words, or hinkity pinkitys, three syllable rhyming words.

May Play

Hink Pinks are two rhyming one-syllable words. Examples of hink pinks are: fat cat, rhyme time, and green scene.

Use the clues below to come up with hink pinks that have a plant name as part of the answer.

1. a tall plant home for buzzing animals   <u>bee tree</u>

2. pink stockings

3. a freezing mother

4. opposite of a wild fire

5. vegetation twine that's okay

6. an evergreen that needs tightening

7. a grim leafy plant

8. a female made from Kentucky Blue

9. to throw tiny green plants

10. petal bandit

Write your own clues and hink pinks on any subject .

11. _____

12. _____

13. _____

14. _____

Name _____ Date _____

Seasonal Activities for Classroom Creativity

Hurrah For The Red, White, And Blue

This activity gives students an opportunity to practice using **research skills** as they search for the meaning behind the colors and symbols of the American flag. They will also have to use **originality** and **imagination** to come up with their own ideas about what these colors and symbols could mean.

Provide a copy or picture of the 1776 American flag for the students. You could also draw a quick sketch on the chalkboard. Ask students what they think the thirteen stars signify. They will most likely come up with the thirteen original colonies as an answer. This will give them a start on the assignment.

Completing the research part of the assignment can be done as small group work, while the students do the bottom part of the assignment independently.

When the assignment is completed, discuss what students found in the research section. Then let students share their favorite response for the independent section of the work.

Hurrah For The Red, White, And Blue

June 14th is Flag Day and we see flags flying everywhere. America's flag is red, white, and blue and has stars and stripes. The colors and symbols were not chosen at random; there was a reason behind each choice.

Do some research to discover the meaning behind the colors and symbols in the original 1776 American flag.

1. Red—

2. White—

3. Blue—

4. Stars—

5. Stripes—

Now use your imagination and give each of those colors and symbols a new meaning.

1. Red—

2. White—

3. Blue—

4. Stars—

5. Stripes—

Name _____ Date _____

Seasonal Activities for Classroom Creativity

"In Your Opinion, Ms. Ross..."

The activity will require **flexibility, imagination,** and **originality** as students consider the idea of the American flag from Betsy Ross's point of view. They will pretend they are interviewing her about the flag designs that she rejected.

It would be worthwhile to point out from the very beginning that the story about Betsy Ross and the first American flag is most likely just that—a story. Along with many other stories that get handed down from generation to generation, it personalizes an event about which we really know few facts. For the sake of this assignment, we are going to pretend that the story is accurate.

This could be a time for the students to see if they can think of any other stories in history that may not be totally accurate:
- Columbus discovering America
- Washington throwing a dollar across the Potomac

Share some of the interviews at the completion of the assignment.

Some flag rejects could be illustrated and included in a bulletin board about the U.S. flag.

"In Your Opinion, Ms. Ross…"

One story credits Betsy Ross with making the first American flag. The upper left hand corner of that flag had a circle of white stars on a blue field. The rest of the flag was made up of red and white horizontal stripes.

Your assignment from the editor of the paper, for which you write, is to interview Betsy Ross. You are to find out what her second choice for the flag design was. Describe the second choice design, and explain why she rejected it. Your findings can be written in any format you choose.

_____

_____

_____

_____

_____

_____

_____

_____

_____

_____

_____

_____

_____

_____

_____

_____

_____

_____

Name _____ Date _____

Seasonal Activities for Classroom Creativity

To Dream Of Summer

This activity encourages students to daydream and use their **imaginations,** while they consider what they like best about summer. They must be **flexible,** and find ways to make these good feelings of summer last throughout the rest of the year. There could also be some **risk taking** involved if the students share some private thoughts with others.

After reading over the assignment with students, take a few minutes to allow students to get into the proper frame of mind. Have them close their eyes, relax, and picture summer. Help them along with a few rhetorical questions: What are they hearing? What are they seeing? What are they doing? What are they feeling?

Share a part of yourself with the students and paint a word picture for them about one of your favorite parts of summer. *I'm lying on a blanket under a tree. The sky is blue with lots of fluffy clouds, and I feel a slight breeze. I hear birds chirping in the trees, and I can hear a little rustling in the grass. I can smell a freshly mown lawn, and it smells wonderful. I look up occasionally at the world around me, but mostly I'm just reading a mystery. It's not a book I have to read, but one I want to read. I feel relaxed and peaceful.*

After students have finished writing, let them share a few of their favorite parts of summer. Then move on to the harder part of the activity: how can we keep summer with us? The ideas students share may give way to some reflective thinking.

To Dream of Summer

Summer officially begins during the month of June. Students and teachers alike can't help but daydream about those wonderful days of summer.

What are three (3) things that you like the most about summer?

1. _____

2. _____

3. _____

How could you incorporate those three things into the rest of the year, and keep the activities and memories of summer with you for a longer time?

_____

_____

_____

_____

_____

_____

_____

_____

_____

_____

_____

_____

_____

_____

_____

Name _____ Date _____

Seasonal Activities for Classroom Creativity

Rewriting The Present

This activity encourages students to expand their **research skills**. This also involves **flexibility** and **complexity**; students are challenged to look at America from a different perspective.

In addition to research about the Revolutionary War, it might be helpful for students to consider other countries that were once British colonies, such as Canada and India. How are these countries different from the U.S.?

This will be a good activity to share with each other. Discussions that spring from answers could be very interesting. There are a variety of answers that the students might have. Several answers could involve governing and government: *Parliament (House of Commons, House of Lords), Prime Minister, different electoral processes, etc. How many students think of ideas that include language, food, clothing, culture, religion, or relations with other countries (for example: Ireland)?*

Rewriting The Present

The 4th of July is called Independence Day, because it is a celebration of the colonies' Declaration of Independence from Great Britain. American independence, however, was not won in a day. It took years and many lives before the colonies actually gained their freedom from British rule.

How different would our lives be today if we were still a part of the British Empire? Some reading and research on the War for Independence might be helpful, as you consider the possibilities.

List and explain below five (5) ways in which our lives would be different if what we know as the United States of America did not exist, and this land was still a British colony.

1. _____

_____

_____

2. _____

_____

_____

3. _____

_____

_____

4. _____

_____

_____

5. _____

_____

_____

Name _____ Date _____

Seasonal Activities for Classroom Creativity

Sing A Song Of Summer

Originality and **imagination** are major aspects of this assignment. Some **risk taking** can occur if students share some of their compositions.

Try some first lines together to keep children from being overwhelmed. How about: Shimmer, shimmer shining sun or Swimming, biking, lots of fun to the tune of *Twinkle, Twinkle Little Star*?

Expect some humming going on during the course of this assignment. It's not easy to do quietly.

This activity could also be done with partners. If you get too many people working on it, the activity can become one- or two-sided and quiet group members can be left out.

Only students who feel comfortable sharing with the class should do so. However, if a couple of students or a group sing their song, it will make sharing easier.

Sing A Song Of Summer

Summer is a wonderful time—no school, plenty of time to rest and relax, play, stay up late, or do whatever tickles your fancy. What a life! It almost makes you want to sing!

Think of all the things you like about summer, and then make up a summer song to express your thoughts. Take the tune of your summer song from the tune of an old nursery rhyme song such as *Twinkle, Twinkle, Little Star*, *Mary Had a Little Lamb*, *London Bridge*, or any other that you remember.

Name _____ Date _____

Seasonal Activities for Classroom Creativity

"Able To Leap Tall Buildings In A Single Bound"

Students will use **imagination** and **originality** as they create their own super heroes and heroines. **Elaboration** will also come into play as students expand on their basic understanding of super heroes and heroines.

Prepare for this assignment and practice **fluency** by having students brainstorm as many super heroes and heroines as they can. These can be listed on the board. You might also make a list of all the *super* things that these characters can do. This prewriting experience will help students prepare for writing about their own super heroes. They may also be able to piggyback some of the ideas listed on the board.

If students are having trouble with the idea of putting *summer* into their character, try creating a character together for autumn.

> **Name:** Leafman
> **Costume:** Wears black tights and leotard with a gold/brown leaf emblem on the front, a gold cape, a gold mask
> **Characteristics:** Drives a leafmobile, chases people who despoil the environment by polluting

Students may want to illustrate their super heroes and heroines and share their drawings along with their descriptions.

The class could vote on their favorites, and a couple of these characters could be enlarged to go on a bulletin board. If you provide large paper doll like figures or patterns of figures for the children to use, it will simplify the project.

"Able To Leap Tall Buildings In A Single Bound"

Super heroes and heroines of every variety fill our comic books with excitement, action, and adventure. These characters face challenges we mere mortals can only imagine.

Create a super hero or heroine of your own. Name the character, give a physical description of the character, and describe your character's powers. Your super hero or heroine should have *some aspect of summer* **(sun, heat, humidity, water sports, mosquitoes, etc.) in its character.**

_____

_____

_____

_____

_____

_____

_____

_____

_____

_____

_____

_____

_____

_____

_____

_____

_____

_____

Name _____ Date _____

Seasonal Activities for Classroom Creativity

How Can It Be August Already?

Students have the opportunity to practice **fluency** with this activity as they list items. Asked to reflect on their summer and what they had expected their summer to be, they will use **curiosity** and their **imaginations** to daydream.

This assignment could be extended to consider what students would like to do next summer, adding a dimension of planning for the future to the reflection of the past.

Ask students to rank a list of ten things they hoped to do this summer, according to a jointly decided upon value (for example: importance, frivolousness, healthiness, pleasure, etc.).

A bulletin board could be titled GRAPHING OUT SUMMER. The bulletin board can include bars labeled nutrition, exercise, culture, travel, fun, etc. On small pieces of paper (that make up the bars), students write information about their summer that fits into the appropriate category. For instance, James might write on one piece of paper that goes in the nutrition bar: *James—planted and took care of two tomato plants.* James might have nothing to put in the travel bar, but could write in the exercise bar the following: *James—went swimming once a week.*

How Can It Be August Already?

How can it be August already? It seems as if summer has just begun, and somehow it's happened again. We haven't done all the fun things, the healthy things, and the things that would make us better people that we wanted and planned to do before we return to school.

List below ten (10) things you hoped to do this summer. Next to each thing, tell whether you accomplished it or not.

1. _____

2. _____

3. _____

4. _____

5. _____

6. _____

7. _____

8. _____

9. _____

10. _____

Name _____ Date _____

Seasonal Activities for Classroom Creativity

A Holiday For August

Students will need to be **curious** and **original** as they consider different ideas for a holiday in August. They will also use **elaboration** as they develop the details for their holiday.

Approach this activity by asking students to brainstorm what they know about the month of August. Ideas should be listed on the board; students can refer to them later.

Divide students into small groups and let them do research in the library, if possible, or bring books into the classroom that they can use. They can research the words August, summer, vacation, or whatever they feel might help them expand their knowledge base for the assignment.

After completing the activity and sharing ideas, students can construct a large calendar page for the bulletin board. Holiday names can be written on the appropriate blocks and illustrations added to make the board more colorful.

A Holiday for August

August has no major holidays in it. Not that we hold that against the month, but wouldn't it be great to have a big holiday right before school starts?

It is up to you to create a holiday for August. It needs to be a holiday that will finish the summer with a flourish. Name the holiday, give it a date, and explain why we celebrate it at that time.

_____

_____

_____

_____

_____

_____

_____

_____

_____

_____

_____

_____

_____

_____

_____

_____

_____

_____

Name _____ Date _____

Seasonal Activities for Classroom Creativity

Alphabetizing Summer

Students improve their **flexibility** as they wrack their brains trying to come up with an **original** word to suit each category. Requesting multiple responses could also practice **fluency**.

This activity can be turned into a game if you put a time limit on its completion, and give points for unduplicated responses. Extra points can also be given to anyone who has a reasonable response for all letters (requires teacher flexibility).

If students enjoy this activity, there are commercially available games which employ some of the same creative thinking skills.

Students can also create their own game boards for a variety of categories.

Alphabetizing Summer

The alphabet is listed below. **Place a word that reminds you of summer in some way next to the letter that begins the word.**

A _____

B _____   O _____

C _____   P _____

D _____   Q _____

E _____   R _____

F irecrackers _____   S _____

G _____   T _____

H _____   U _____

I _____   V _____

J _____   W _____

K _____   X _____

L _____   Y _____

M _____   Z oo visiting _____

N _____

Name _____ Date _____

Seasonal Activities for Classroom Creativity

To Celebrate Work

Students use **fluency** as they generate numerous responses. **Curiosity** is also involved as students think reflectively in their exploration of personal feelings about their futures. Students will need to **elaborate** as they expand upon their ideas.

One way to jump start student thinking is to allow the whole class to brainstorm a list of professions. Put a time limit on the brainstorming, and remind the students that they can piggyback ideas already presented (for example: farmer, citrus farmer, dairy farmer, grocery story owner, clerk in a grocery store, etc.).

Another approach would be for you to discuss different professions you considered at various points of your life. Ask the class why they think the different professions might have appealed to you.

You may want to point out that school counselors and librarians can be helpful with this subject. They are good resources themselves and can also point you to useful books (for example: a dictionary of occupational titles, books on specific professions, etc.).

To Celebrate Work

Labor Day is a holiday celebrated on the first Monday of September. It was created to honor working men and women. One day each of us will take our place in the world of work. Maybe you will be so pleased with your choice of profession that you will want to celebrate your choice too.

It's never too soon to dream about the type of profession you might like to have. **List below three professions in which you have an interest, and then explain what it is about each profession that interests you.**

Profession #1 and Explanation: _____

_____

_____

_____

_____

Profession #2 and Explanation: _____

_____

_____

_____

_____

Profession #3 and Explanation: _____

_____

_____

_____

_____

Name _____ Date _____

Seasonal Activities for Classroom Creativity

School Similes

In this exercise, students practice **flexibility** as they explore new ways to look at common school related experiences. Students use **originality** as they look for novel ways of completing the similes. Students will also participate in **risk taking**, because some of the items involve feelings they may not have shared with others before they do this activity.

Since most students at this age have had little experience with similes, it would be helpful to discuss the *word pictures* similes try to create. Compare similes: *as soft as velvet* and *as soft as the velvet fur of a new puppy* or *as white as snow* and *as white as a snowy blanket covering the world*. Which phrase in each of these pairs creates better word pictures? Why?

Introduce students to the word *trite*, which *The American Heritage Dictionary* defines as "overused and commonplace; lacking interest or originality." Practice writing similes together avoiding trite and obvious responses. You might use the following:

> as black as . . .
> as quiet as . . .
> shiny like . . .
> as short as . .
> angry like . . .

Let students create a *Class Book of Similes* using a spiral notebook or binder. Each page of the book might include the following entries:

> Simile—
> Where found—
> Finder—
> Comments—
>   (good word picture, trite, easy or difficult to understand, etc.)

Near the end of the school year, students can discuss which similes they felt were the most descriptive and which were their favorites.

School Similes

A simile is a figure of speech in which one thing is compared to another entirely different thing by the use of the words *like* or *as*. Examples of similes are: *the puppy felt like a velvet pillow* or *the room was as noisy as a parakeet cage at a pet store*.

September is the month when our thoughts return to another year of school. **Complete the similes below to help describe how you feel about school. All your responses should be related to school.**

1. The first day of school is like . . . _____
   _____

2. New discoveries are as much fun as. . . _____
   _____

3. Classmates are like. . . _____
   _____

4. Tests can be as scary as. . . _____
   _____

5. A teacher is like. . . _____
   _____

6. A good grade on a paper is as exciting as. . . _____
   _____

7. Homework is like. . . _____
   _____

8. Problems at school are as painful as. . . _____
   _____

9. The school bus is like. . . _____
   _____

10. The library is as peaceful as. . . _____
    _____

Name _____ Date _____

Seasonal Activities for Classroom Creativity

Naming The Seasons

"Naming the Seasons" requires **flexibility** from students as they look at seasonal names in different ways. **Imagination** and **originality** are also used as students seek alternative answers.

A discussion of the meaning of the following quote from Shakespeare's *Romeo and Juliet* would be a good starting place for this activity:

> *What's in a name? That which we call a rose*
> *By any other name would smell as sweet.*

How important are the names we give people and things? Do names color our perceptions? Brainstorm examples of words that sound negative or give off a negative connotation (for example: pond scum, yucky, putrid, nauseous, noxious, etc.).

Students can share and discuss their choices after completing the activity. They can then vote on which names would be the most effective substitutes for the present names of the seasons.

Develop a survey that lists students' top choices of new names for each season. After totals from the survey have been tabulated, students can collectively write a report that shows the results.

Naming The Seasons

We use the term *fall* interchangeably with the word *autumn* to describe the season that occurs between summer and winter. *Fall* is a verb that becomes a noun when we use it as a season. Why do you think *fall* is used to describe this season?

Choose two (2) words that could be used as names for each of the seasons *and* explain why you made these choices.

SPRING

1. _____
_____

2. _____
_____

SUMMER

1. _____
_____

2. _____
_____

AUTUMN

1. Fall _____
_____

2. _____
_____

WINTER

1. _____
_____

2. _____
_____

Name _____ Date _____

Seasonal Activities for Classroom Creativity

A Day Of Your Own

For this activity, students are challenged to use **originality** and **elaboration** as they create and describe their own holiday. They also use **imagination** as they explore what it is about themselves that deserves a personal holiday.

Give students an idea of what you'd like from this assignment by letting the class come up with ideas of someone they know who could have a holiday of their own: a favorite teacher, a local athlete, a local politician, or someone in the arts. Ask students to talk about why this individual deserves a holiday. What sets this individual apart from other people? What qualities do they have that are admirable?

Students can take the assignment further and decide how their holiday should be celebrated—fireworks, food, music, presents, etc. Who would celebrate their holiday? Would they be willing to share their holiday with someone else or should this be their day alone? How important should their holiday be compared to other holidays?

A Day Of Your Own

National Children's Day occurs in October, Mother's Day is in May, Father's Day is in June, and Grandparent's Day is in September. Maybe it is time you had a day of your very own.

Choose a date for Your Day, decide what it should be called, give an explanation as to why you deserve a day to celebrate YOU, and tell why others should celebrate YOU too.

_____

_____

_____

_____

_____

_____

_____

_____

_____

_____

_____

_____

_____

_____

_____

_____

_____

_____

Name _____ Date _____

Seasonal Activities for Classroom Creativity

A Historical Halloween

Students must be **original** and **flexible** as they approach the idea of a Halloween costume from different perspectives. **Complexity** will come into play as they challenge themselves not to be satisfied with obvious solutions. Students will have to use their **imaginations** as they seek alternatives.

If students find the scope of the idea a little daunting, you might narrow the choices. Designate a period in history from which they must choose, or divide the class into two groups—one group dressed as historical figures from the 1700s and the other group dressed as figures from the 1800s.

After students have completed the assignment, ask them to illustrate one of their choices. Their illustrations could be kept simple or combined with different media to form a collage.

Individual student illustrations can be displayed on a bulletin board. Or students could vote on four or five of their favorite choices, and form groups to make larger collage-type examples of the costumes for display.

A Historical Halloween

You are invited to a Historical Halloween Party where you dress as a figure from history. Think creatively and be flexible as you consider your choices. Instead of going as George Armstrong Custer or Sitting Bull, think about going as a prairie dog that had a ringside seat at Custer's Last Stand.

Make two (2) choices of possible costumes. Write your choices and then explain why you'd be interested in dressing as this figure in history.

Choice #1 and Explanation: _____

_____

_____

_____

_____

_____

_____

_____

Choice #2 and Explanation: _____

_____

_____

_____

_____

_____

_____

_____

_____

Name _____ Date _____

Seasonal Activities for Classroom Creativity

Originality At Halloween

Students are asked to be **fluent** and **original** as they come up with a list of *interesting* words that can be used in a Halloween story. **Curiosity** can lead students to discover different avenues for finding these interesting words.

Get students started on this assignment by asking the class to decide upon five words that might be *overused* in a Halloween story. Another approach would be for the class to develop a list of interesting words for a Christmas story, a story about puppies, or anything else that interests students.

When students have completed their list, ask them to choose their five most interesting words. Have them write a Halloween paragraph using three of their five words. What are some dull, overused words they could have used in place of the three they used? Why were their choices better?

Ask your students to copy their paragraphs neatly to mount on black or orange paper. Add a few paper ghosts or spiders and put paragraphs on display.

Originality At Halloween

Sometimes when we write, our originality and creativity take a short vacation. When this happens, we get stuck using the same old dull, boring words that lots of other people use. These are words that are trite and hackneyed. They have no power to interest a reader, because they have been overused and repeated too frequently. A good example of a word that has no novelty or interest because of overuse is *nice*.

Imagine that you will be writing a Halloween story that will fascinate readers and make them want to read more. **Make a list below of interesting words that can be used in your story. AVOID TRITE, OVERUSED WORDS!**

Name _____ Date _____

Seasonal Activities for Classroom Creativity

Presidential Qualities

The multiple responses students are asked to provide for this assignment encourages **fluency**. The reflective thinking in this activity requires **curiosity** and **complexity**.

In general, students of this age do not have their own political beliefs, but tend to profess their parents' beliefs. It's important to recognize that this assignment is *not* about politics. This is not about a particular candidate or political party. It is about the make-up of a person's character and can be kept at that level without reference to individuals.

To prepare for the activity, students brainstorm a list of qualities they want in a friend. A second list could be made of qualities they feel parents or teachers should have. Which of these listed qualities might carry over to the presidency? There may be others that weren't listed. Is there something special you need to have to be president or are we looking at qualities we'd like to see in all of us?

After completing the assignment, determine which five *most important qualities* received the greatest interest from students. Look back in history and get a consensus of opinion on a historical figure that best exhibits each of the five qualities (for example: George Washington's honesty, Abe Lincoln's persistence, etc.).

Presidential Qualities

The United States holds a presidential election every fourth year on the first Tuesday after the first Monday in November. This has occurred every four years since the first election in 1788.

Each voter goes to the polling place hoping that his or her choice will win and that the new president will have all the characteristics needed to do a great job. Not everyone agrees which characteristics are important in the person we elect as president. **List below the five (5) most important qualities you feel a president should have. Explain your reasoning for each.**

Quality #1 and Reasoning: _____

_____

_____

Quality #2 and Reasoning: _____

_____

_____

Quality #3 and Reasoning: _____

_____

_____

Quality #4 and Reasoning: _____

_____

_____

Quality #5 and Reasoning: _____

_____

_____

Name _____ Date _____

Seasonal Activities for Classroom Creativity

A Nontraditional Thanksgiving

Students will use **flexibility** when they look at Thanksgiving dinner in a different way. **Curiosity** and **complexity** are also involved as students explore dinner choices and seek alternative ethnic foods.

This assignment could be a large or small group activity as well as an individual activity.

Students can brainstorm a list of favorite foods, and then research the ethnicity of these foods.

Another approach to the assignment would be to divide the U.S. into geographic sections, which can then be researched for a variety of food styles.

Drawings or magazine illustrations of the completed menu can be compiled and displayed.

It would also be fun to create and taste test some of the different food dishes in the menus.

A Nontraditional Thanksgiving

Family traditions help to determine how we celebrate specific holidays. A traditional Thanksgiving dinner for one family might seem very strange to another family.

Plan a nontraditional Thanksgiving dinner below. It should include a variety of foods that reveal the ethnic diversity of the United States. Beside each food choice, indicate which region of the country, ethnic group, or culture that particular food represents.

Name _____ Date _____

Seasonal Activities for Classroom Creativity

Counting Our Blessings

Fluency is a major component of this exercise as students are asked to count their blessings in different ways. Students will also be using their **imaginations** to provide a variety of responses.

It is often easier to enumerate wrongs done to us or failings in others and in ourselves than it is to focus on the positives in our world. This activity furnishes students with an opportunity to look at the pluses in their lives.

The third section of the activity, which asks for a list of things for which you'd like to be thankful, provides a chance to extend the activity: How realistic were your choices? What steps could be taken to make each of your choices come true? Are your choices dependent upon your actions alone or upon others too? What would be necessary to convince others to join you in a common goal?

This activity could easily be turned into a bulletin board with all students contributing.

Counting Our Blessings

We all have a lot for which we can be thankful, and we do not always take the time to remember these blessings.

See how fluent you can be by following the directions below.

List five (5) things for which you are thankful:

1. _____
2. _____
3. _____
4. _____
5. _____

List five (5) things about which you're glad you *don't* have to worry:

1. _____
2. _____
3. _____
4. _____
5. _____

List five (5) things for which you would like to be thankful:

1. _____
2. _____
3. _____
4. _____
5. _____

Name _____ Date _____

Seasonal Activities for Classroom Creativity

Winter Couplets

For this activity, students must be **flexible** as they express their thoughts in rhymes. This activity also involves students using their **imaginations** and being **original** as they write their couplets.

This is an opportunity for students to discover that poems can be as short as one couplet long. Ogden Nash wrote some delightful couplet-long poems that appeal to children of all ages. Here are two that can be found in Nash's book *Zoo*, published by Stewart, Tabori & Chang:

The Cow
The cow is of the bovine ilk;
One end is moo, the other, milk.

The Fly
The Lord in His wisdom made the fly
And then forgot to tell us why.

The rhythm of the couplets is most important and should be stressed rather than counting syllables. Concentrating on the exact number of syllables needed in a line can stifle creativity. Reading the couplets out loud helps students recognize which lines match or don't match rhythmically without resorting to counting syllables.

Animals are a good topic for practice, and the class can work together to write some couplets.

After writing their three couplets about snow, students can gather in small groups to combine some of their couplets into a poem of several lines. The poem should make sense, so they'll have to attend to the content as well as the rhyme.

Display completed poems in the classroom, so everyone has a chance to see themselves as poets.

Winter Couplets

A couplet is two rhyming lines of verse. Although it is important to keep the number of syllables in each line of a couplet similar, it is not essential that they be exact. It is most important that the rhythm of the lines sound well together. Related couplets can be combined in a logical sequence to form a poem.

Example:

Winter Fun?

The gray winter sky looks so dreary
As I peer from eyes that are teary.

My poor arms are already aching,
And my back is certainly breaking.

I can no longer feel all my toes,
Need a tissue for my drippy nose,

And I am sure my lungs are frozen.
Before a fire I could be dozin'.

THIS DRIVEWAY LOOKS FIVE MILES LONG!

Write three (3) couplets about snow. Be sure to check that the two lines in each couplet rhyme and that the number of syllables per line is similar.

_____

_____

_____

_____

_____

_____

_____

_____

_____

_____

Name _____ Date _____

Seasonal Activities for Classroom Creativity

Winter Acrostics

For this activity, **flexibility** is needed, because students, in general, have very little experience with writing a poem that has vertical as well as horizontal requirements. Students will need to use their **imaginations** and be **original**. **Complexity** is also involved in this activity as students face the challenge of finding alternatives to fit each of the letters.

Practice, before actually beginning the activity, helps put students into the right frame of mind. Try some acrostics on the board together. Your topics might include: ANTS, GAMES, WATER, WISHES, or PLANS.

It should be stressed that there has to be some sense to the acrostic. There should be an obvious "flow" from line to line. The acrostic does not have to be read consecutively as a sentence, although it can be.

Acrostics do not need to be titled, although students might like to do so. The vertical word can also serve as the title.

After acrostics are completed and shared, mount them on blue or black construction paper. Add cut-out snowflakes, mittens, scarves, or boots, and you have a bulletin board.

Winter Acrostics

An acrostic is a form of unrhymed verse in which a word is written vertically, and each letter in the word becomes the beginning letter in a line of verse.

Example:

Can't find my mittens
Or my boots.
Like to go outside in the snow,
Don't think Mom will let me.

Write an acrostic below using WINTER as the topic. When you finish, write another acrostic on the back of this page using one of the following as your topic word: ICICLE, FRIGID, SNOWBALL, SLIPPERY, or FROST.

**W
I
N
T
E
R**

Name _____ Date _____

Seasonal Activities for Classroom Creativity

Holiday Gifts

The list students make in this activity will give them practice with **fluency.** They will **elaborate** on their ideas as they give the reasons for their choices. **Risk taking** is involved as students defend their choices and share with others.

Ask students to take out a piece of scratch paper, and write down three gifts they'd like. Then ask them how they would explain to someone else why they should have one of the gifts.

Have students do the same thing with three gifts for their family (or their town or state) in order to broaden their thinking.

This activity extends the gift giving idea to a larger context than is normally considered. What would you like to give the whole world? What does the world need?

Share choices when the activity is completed. Which choices were the most common? Was there a gift that someone else thought of giving that you wish you'd chosen?

Holiday Gifts

You have been given an amazing opportunity; one that will require considerable thought and reasoning. By some strange twist of fate you have been chosen to select five holiday gifts for the world.

List below the five (5) gifts you will give and your reasoning for giving each gift.

Gift #1 _____

_____

_____

Gift #2 _____

_____

_____

Gift #3 _____

_____

_____

Gift #4 _____

_____

_____

Gift #5 _____

_____

_____

Name _____ Date _____

Seasonal Activities for Classroom Creativity